## DATE DUE

The Military Life of

# GUSTAVUS ADOLPHUS

## FATHER OF MODERN WAR

by TREVOR NEVITT DUPUY
Col., U.S. Army, Ret.

FRANKLIN WATTS, INC.
575 Lexington Avenue
New York, N.Y. 10022

14235

SBN 531-01878-4

Copyright © 1969 by Franklin Watts, Inc.
Library of Congress Catalog Card Number: 79-77239
Printed in the United States of America

1  2  3  4  5  6  7

TELL ME WHY, TELL ME HOW

# WHY DO WE SEE RAINBOWS?

## MELISSA STEWART

mc **Marshall Cavendish**
Benchmark
New York

Marshall Cavendish Benchmark
99 White Plains Road
Tarrytown, NY 10591-5502
www.marshallcavendish.us

Library of Congress Cataloging-in-Publication Data

Stewart, Melissa.
  Why do we see rainbows? / by Melissa Stewart.
      p. cm.—(Tell me why, tell me how)
  Summary: "Provides comprehensive information on how the human eye sees
color"—Provided by publisher.
  Includes index.
  ISBN 978-0-7614-2919-7
  1.  Color vision—Juvenile literature. 2.  Color—Juvenile literature.
  3. Rainbow—Juvenile literature.  I. Title. II. Series.

  QP483.S735 2009
  612.8'4—dc22

  2007024628

Photo research by Candlepants Incorporated

Cover Photo: Wojtek Buss / Art Life Images

The photographs in this book are used by permission and through the courtesy of:
*Shutterstock*: 1, 25. *Corbis*: Ariel Skelley, 4; W. Cody, 6; Robert Llewellyn, 13; Peter M. Fisher, 15; Jim Craigmyle,
16; So Hing-Keung, 19. *age fotostock*: David Muscroft, 5; Mark Turner, 22; Craig Tuttle, 24. *Photo Researchers Inc.*:
Gusto Productions, 8; Véronique Estiot, 9; Dr. John Brackenbury, 18. *Alamy Images*: Phototake Inc., 10.
*PhotoTakeUSA.com*: Pr. P. Sole, 12. *Peter Arnold Inc.*: Hympendahl, 14. *Getty Images*: Richard Wahlstrom, 20;
Gary Yeowell, 23.

Editor: Joy Bean
Publisher: Michelle Bisson
Art Director: Anahid Hamparian
Series Designer: Alex Ferrari

Printed in Malaysia
1 3 5 6 4 2

# CONTENTS

A playground is full of color, from green monkey bars to red shirts and blue jeans.

# A World of Color

The next time you go outside for recess, take a look around. What do you see? Above you is a blue sky full of puffy, white clouds. Green grass grows in the rich, brown soil below you. Your classmates are kicking red rubber balls across hard, black pavement. The world around you is full of color.

You can probably name ten or twenty different colors, but your eyes can see many more. They can see about two million different shades of color. Your eyes know that your favorite worn blue jeans are not exactly the same color as your friend's dark blue T-shirt. They also have no trouble telling the difference between the pinkish red, orangey red, and brownish red.

Being able to see colors helps people

These girls are eating a lollipop with all the colors of the rainbow.

5

stay safe. You know that a red traffic light means stop and a green traffic light means go. The color of a banana tells you whether it is ripe or rotten. If you spot a bee's black and yellow stripes, you know that you should slowly back away.

Your eyes could not do their job without light from the Sun. The Sun is a star—a giant ball of boiling gases. Life on Earth could not survive without energy from the Sun. Waves of light energy race through space at about 186,000 miles (299,000 kilometers) per second. At that speed, sunlight reaches Earth in about eight minutes.

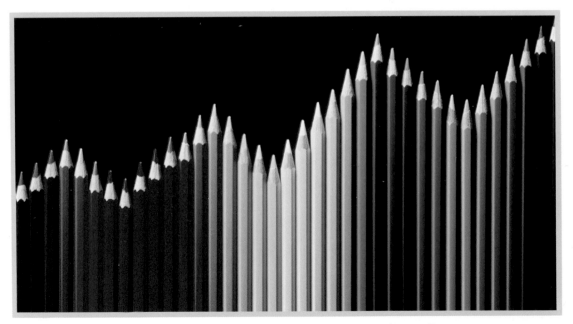

Look at all the shades of color you can see in these colored pencils.

Waves of light energy are shaped just like waves of water. Each wave has a high point called a peak and a low point called a trough. The distance between two peaks is called the **wavelength**.

Now I Know!
What do your eyes need in order to see?
Light

The Sun gives off many different kinds of energy. Some of that energy has short wavelengths, and some of it has long wavelengths. Most energy wavelengths are invisible to the human eye, but you can see some of the Sun's light energy. Scientists call the wavelengths of energy that people can see **visible light**. Visible light is what allows you to see colors when you look at the sky, the ground, and the red rubber ball at recess.

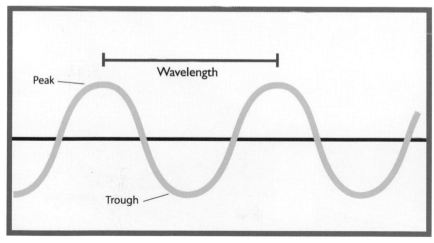

A wavelength is the distance between the peaks of two waves.

If you have never taken a close look at your eyeball, now is your chance.

# Inside Your Eyes

When you look at your face in a mirror, you can only see a little bit of each eyeball. Most of it is hidden below your skin.

The first thing most people notice when they look at your eye is the colorful **iris**. It can be blue, brown, green, hazel, or even violet. The black dot in the center of your iris is an opening called the **pupil**.

Waves of light enter your eye through the pupil. Then they pass through the **lens**. The lens is a clear, rubbery layer of tissue. When muscles surrounding your lens stretch or relax, they

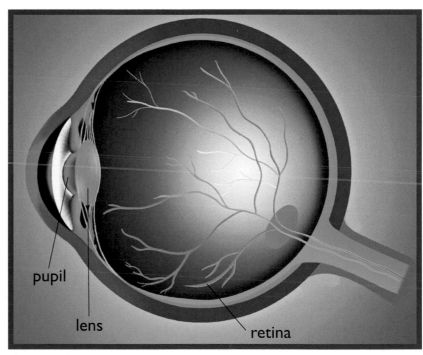

This is what the inside of our eyeball looks like. Light passes through your pupil and lens then hits your retina.

9

change its shape. That is how your eyes bring objects into focus.

Finally, the Sun's light waves strike the **retina**, a thin layer of tissue that lines the back of your eyeball. Most of your retina is covered with light sensors called **rods** and **cones**. These special cells sense waves of visible light.

More than one hundred million rod cells are packed along the edges of your retina. These straight, thin light sensors go to work at night. They help you see

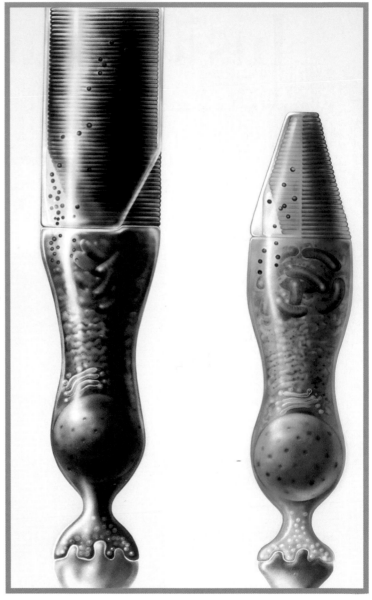

This drawing of a rod cell (left) and a cone cell (right) shows the shapes they are named for.

10

shapes and detect movement in the dark.

During the day, six million cone cells let you see the world in full color. These light sensors are shaped like upside-down ice cream cones. They line the center of your retina.

Your eyes contain three different kinds of cones. Each one is tuned into certain wavelengths of visible light. Blue cones are best at detecting blue light, which has a short wavelength. Green cones are best at detecting green light, which has a medium wavelength. Red cones are best at detecting red light, which has a long wavelength.

Now I Know!

Name the light-sensing cells in your eyes that help you see colors.

Cones.

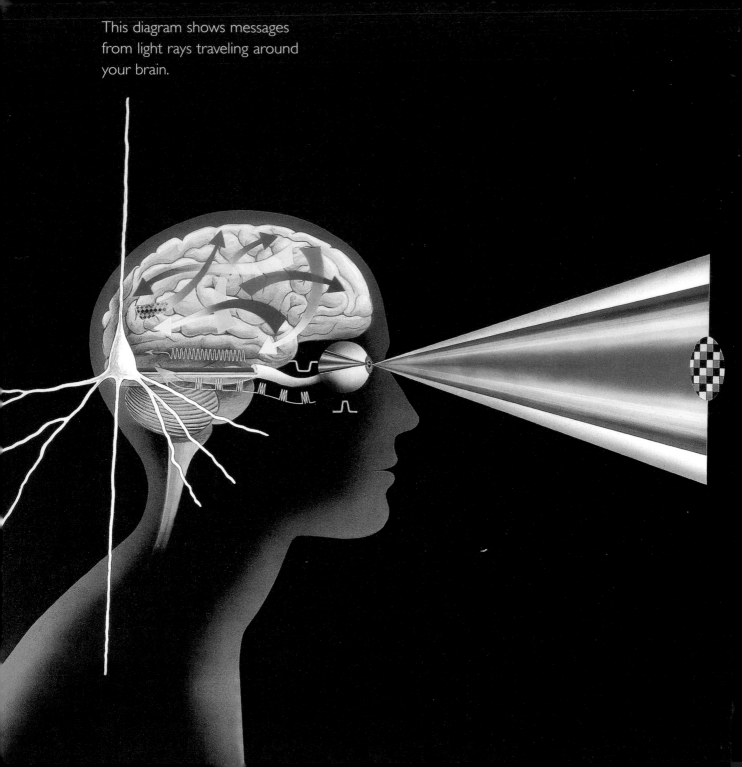

This diagram shows messages from light rays traveling around your brain.

# How You See Colors

Light energy from the Sun contains short, medium, and long wavelengths of visible light. When sunlight hits your eyes directly, all three kinds of cones send messages to your brain. Your brain combines those messages and tells you that the light is white. White light is a mixture of all the colors.

Imagine white sunlight hitting an object, such as a tree. The tree **absorbs**, or takes in, some of the light. The rest of the light bounces back, or gets **reflected**, into your eyes.

When sunlight hits these trees, the leaves reflect the colors of autumn into your eyes.

The paint on a red car absorbs the short (blue) wavelengths and medium (green) wavelengths of the Sun's visible light. It reflects the long (red) wavelengths. When the long (red) wavelengths strike the retina in your eye, the cones that detect red light send messages to your brain. The cones

This bright red car sends your red-detecting cone cells into overdrive.

that detect green and blue light do not send messages. Finally, your brain tells you that the car is red.

The sky looks blue because it reflects short blue wavelengths of light and absorbs all the other wavelengths of visible light. Grass looks green because it reflects green light into your eyes and absorbs all the other colors.

The sky looks blue and the grass looks green because they reflect some wavelengths of visible light and absorb others.

Not everything in the world is blue or green or red, however. To see yellow, purple, and every other color, the cones in your eyes work together. Even though red cones are perfectly tuned into wavelengths of red light, they can also

The sky reflects blue wavelengths of light. Leaves reflect green wavelengths of light, and sunflowers reflect yellow wavelengths. You see yellow wavelengths with your red and green cones.

detect wavelengths that are a little bit shorter and a little bit longer. Green cones and blue cones can also sense a range of light wavelengths.

When sunlight strikes a field of sunflowers, the flowers absorb most of the wavelengths of visible light. They reflect the yellow wavelengths. Yellow wavelengths are a little shorter than red wavelengths and a little longer than green wavelengths. That means both red and green cones can detect yellow wavelengths. Blue cones cannot. When your brain gets a message from your red and green cones but not from your blue cones, you see the color yellow.

The combination of messages your brain receives from your cones determines what color you see. Slight differences in the messages help you tell the difference between lavender and purple, pink and red, and thousands of other colors.

Look carefully at this raindrop hanging from a flower bud. You can see the reflection of a flower in full bloom.

# Inside a Raindrop

You have learned that when light energy from the Sun strikes certain objects, some of the wavelengths are absorbed and some are reflected. Light waves pass straight through some solid materials, however.

Most objects absorb or reflect sunlight, but light rays pass straight through glass.

Glass looks clear and colorless because it does not absorb or reflect light. What happens when visible light waves hit glass? They slow down and bend, or **refract**. The same thing happens when light waves hit falling raindrops.

Inside a raindrop, some wavelengths of visible light slow down and bend more than others. Red light, which has the longest wavelengths, travels the fastest. As a result, it bends the least. Short wavelengths of blue light travel the slowest and bend the most. Because different wavelengths of visible light bend in different amounts, the beam of white sunlight breaks apart and spreads into a band of colors called a **spectrum**.

The most obvious colors in a spectrum are red, orange, yellow, green, blue, and violet. But each of these major colors blends together at the edges to create dozens of other colors that your eyes cannot easily see. When all these colored waves of light strike the back of a raindrop, they are reflected back into the drop. Then they hit the front of the drop and pass into the air. As

A special piece of glass called a prism has a lot in common with a raindrop. Both can bend wavelengths of white light to create a spectrum.

20

light waves move out of a raindrop, they refract for a second time. This causes the wavelengths of colored light to spread out even more, and a rainbow forms.

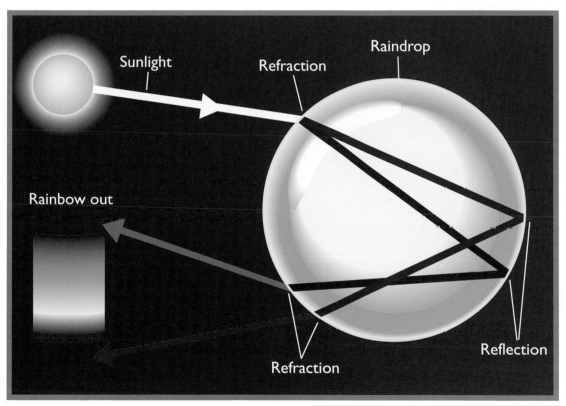

Why does white light separate into a spectrum inside a raindrop? Because different wavelengths of light refract different amounts.

21

It does not have to rain for you to see a rainbow. Any watery spray can create one.

# Why Do We See Rainbows?

Every time it rains, light waves passing through the air are refracted, reflected, and then refracted again by millions of raindrops. Why do we not see a rainbow every time it rains? The conditions have to be just right.

To see a rainbow, the Sun must be shining in one part of the sky and rain must be falling in another part of the sky.

A beautiful rainbow stretches across the sky over the Pass of Glencoe in Scotland.

Your chances of spotting the rainbow are best if the rainy area of the sky is quite dark and the sky directly above you is clear. If you stand with your back toward the Sun and look toward the rain shower, you might see a circular arch of color.

Most of the time, rainbows can only be seen in the early morning or late afternoon, when the sun is low in the sky. A morning rainbow appears when the Sun shines in the east and rain falls in the west. An afternoon rainbow appears

The colors of light in a rainbow blend into one another.

Seeing a full rainbow such as this one is a rare treat.

when the sun shines in the west and rain falls in the east.

A single raindrop does not produce the rainbow that you see stretching across the sky. Even though a raindrop creates a full spectrum of colored light, you can see only some of the light streaming out of it. The color that you see from a particular raindrop depends on your position and the position of the raindrop.

When you look toward a rainstorm, your eyes see long wavelengths of red light refracted from raindrops high in the sky. They see short wavelengths of violet light refracted from raindrops lower in the sky. That is why red always appears at the top of a rainbow and violet always appears at the bottom. The order of the other four colors is also determined by their wavelengths.

Whenever you are lucky enough to see a beautiful rainbow arching across the sky, the colors are always the same: red, orange, yellow, green, blue, and violet.

# Activity

Not all rainbows are caused by rain. You can see rainbows whenever there is a fine mist of water in the air. You might see a rainbow in a waterfall or a fountain. You can even see one in the spray from a garden hose. On the next warm, sunny day, you can try to make your own rainbow. All you will need is a hose with a spray nozzle and a friend to help.

1. Go outside before 9:00 A.M. or after 3:00 P.M., turn on the water and open the spray nozzle on your hose.

2. Adjust the spray nozzle so the water is coming out in a fine mist.

3. Have your friend spray the water high into the air.

4. Stand with the sun behind you and look at the mist

from the hose. You should be able to see a tiny rainbow. It will show up best against a dark background, such as a row of bushes.

5. Take a photograph of the rainbow.

6. Try moving the spray nozzle in different ways. Can you still see the rainbow? Does the rainbow look different? Write down all your observations in a notebook.

# Index

Page numbers for illustrations are in **boldface.**

# Glossary

**absorb**—To take in.

**cone**—Eye cells that help people see colors during the day.

**iris**—A ring-shaped flap of tissue that gives the eye its color.

**lens**—A clear layer of tissue that changes shapes to focus images on the retina.

**pupil**—The circular opening in the center of the iris.

**reflect**—To bounce off.

**refract**—To bend.

**retina**—A thin layer of tissue that lines the back of the eye.

**rod**—Eye cells that detect shapes and movement at night.

**spectrum**—The band of mulitcolored light produced when sunlight is separated by diffraction.

**visible light**—Energy from the Sun that can be detected by the human eye.

**wavelength**—The distance between the peaks of two waves next to each other.

# Find Out More

## BOOKS

Gardner, Robert, and Tom LaBaff. *Dazzling Science Projects with Light and Color.*
    Berkeley Heights, New Jersey: Enslow, 2006.
Parker, Steve. *The Science of Light.* Chicago: Heinemann Library, 2005.

## WEB SITES

Make a Splash with Color

http://www.thetech.org/exhibits/online/color/intro/

Seeing Color

http://askabiologist.asu.edu/research/seecolor/rodsandcones.html

What Is Color?

http://skyserver.sdss.org/dr1/en/proj/advanced/color/whatis.asp#trythis

What Wavelength Goes with a Color?

http://eosweb.larc.nasa.gov/EDDOCS/Wavelengths_for_Colors.html#violet